Musher's Night Before CHRISTMAS

To Reed —
a howlin'
good
boy!

Jamie Brown

Musher's Night Before CHRISTMAS

By Tricia Brown
Illustrated by Debra Dubac

ARF
ARF
ARF

PELICAN PUBLISHING COMPANY
Gretna 2011

To Kelton Patrick, our newest pup, with love—T. B.

To my fierce little leader, Carson, and his winning dog team—
Annie, Onyx and Becca.—D. D.

Copyright © 2011
By Tricia Brown

Illustrations copyright © 2011
By Debra Dubac

Library of Congress Cataloging-in-Publication Data

Brown, Tricia.
  Musher's night before Christmas / Tricia Brown ; illustrated by Debra Dubac.
    p. cm.
  Summary: When Nome, Alaska, is snowed in on Christmas Eve, Santa enlists the aid of a
dog musher who lives on the Iditerod Trail. Includes facts about Alaska and dog sled racing.
  ISBN 978-1-58980-843-0 (hardcover : alk. paper) [1. Stories in rhyme. 2. Christmas—Fiction.
3. Santa Claus—Fiction. 4. Sled dogs—Fiction. 5. Dogs—Fiction. 6. Nome (Alaska)—Fiction.]
I. Dubac, Debbie, ill. II. Title.
  PZ8.3.B81576Mu 2010
  [E]—dc22
                              2010012684

Printed in Singapore
Published by Pelican Publishing Company, Inc.
1000 Burmaster Street, Gretna, Louisiana 70053

'Twas the night before Christmas at the top of the
    world,
And above North Pole, Santa's flag was unfurled,
Shining bright in the darkness, candy-caned red
    and white.
At the sight of its splendor, throngs cheered with
    delight.

Not an elf missed the send-off;
  every year without pause,
They pounded their mittens in
  muffled applause.
Overhead on huge speakers,
  Christmas experts shared
  facts
About rooftops and reindeer,
  their hooves and their racks.

"A little-known fact," one said
  into the mic.
"All reindeer grow antlers,
  male and female alike."
"Unreal!" said the other, his
  voice filled with mirth.
"It's a beautiful night for a run
  'round the earth."

Just then the famed reindeer to the line drew the
  sleigh.
When Santa stepped down, Mrs. Claus came to say,
"The weatherman called. It's whiteout at Nome.
So keep Rudy's nose on and come safely home."

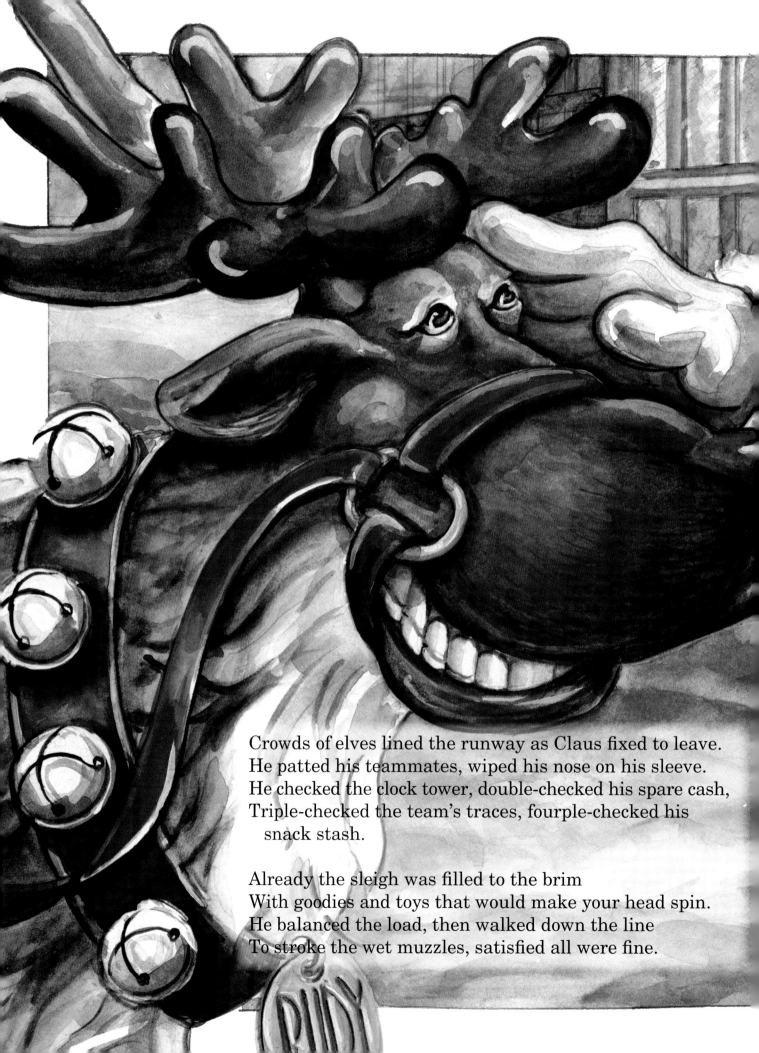

Crowds of elves lined the runway as Claus fixed to leave.
He patted his teammates, wiped his nose on his sleeve.
He checked the clock tower, double-checked his spare cash,
Triple-checked the team's traces, fourple-checked his
    snack stash.

Already the sleigh was filled to the brim
With goodies and toys that would make your head spin.
He balanced the load, then walked down the line
To stroke the wet muzzles, satisfied all were fine.

The reindeer, impatient, trained well for this night.
From his place at the reins, Santa called, "Okay,
  hike!"
Three-two-one! Off they launched, supercharged
  with the thrill
Of delivering Christmas, despite the deep chill.

At a faraway cabin, the dog yard was
   hopping
With huskies a-howling, a-yapping,
   a-popping.
The boss had brought snacks; their bowls
   had been filled.
Soon they'd curl up, their appetites killed.

Fleece booties were hung by the woodstove with
  care,
In hopes that they'd don them ere time to prepare
And train for the Quest and Iditarod races.
Whether leaders or wheel dogs, they wanted first
  places.

The musher's top dogs were the best all around.
They'd pulled Tom up mountains, down trails, and
  to town.
He'd won every dog race, the great ones and small.
With a team that he'd coached through the summer
  and fall.

Well into the night, all were nestled in bed.
Yet the dogs' extra senses said someone in red
Was about to show up and change the whole night
From boring old sleep to adventure-filled flight.

The heavenly peace had been broken already
By the boss in the bunkroom, snoring loudly and steady.
The snow-covered cabin, like a Christmas-card scene,
Yet inside were no presents; this year had been lean.

Now atop their doghouses,
   huskies spied one
   approaching.
A sleigh pulled by reindeer,
   from the sky, was
   encroaching.
The dogs tilted their heads,
   noses up to the moon.
They sang out their welcome,
   a high, mournful tune.

The calls, how they spread, like a
    rumor unstopped,
As onto the rooftop, the team
    downward plopped.
"Gee whiz!" Santa groaned, adding,
    "Oh, what a night!"
In the lead was his Rudolph, with a
    nose not so bright.

Tom scrambled outside,
    shouting, "What is the
    matter?"
Then he looked to the chimney,
    where he'd heard all the
    clatter.
Spying Santa above him, Tom
    asked, "Are you kidding?
I ain't on the nice list. Stopping
    here? Is it fitting?"

"Tom! My dear boy!" Santa laughed,
    "Ho, ho, ho!
It seems you've come out without boots
    in the snow."
It's true, Tom was chilled, his
    stockinged feet prancing.
His mind filled with questions, not the
    dance he was dancing.

"Tom, the job's nearly done, but
    finished we're not.
All the world has its presents, 'cept for
    one lonely spot
On the cold Bering Sea; it's called
    Nome, Alaska.
We couldn't deliver, so a question I'll
    ask ya."

"Rudy's worked hard, but his nose power's spent.
Now with Nome weather-bound, I need your
   consent.
I've followed the news; your dogs have good zip.
So I'm wantin' to know, can *you* make the trip?"

In the wink of an eye, Tom was planning his
  scheme.
Quickly suited and booted, then assembling his team.
From a kennel of champions, Tom chose his best
  eight:
Joe, Lance, Susan, Rick, Doug, Jeff, Martin, Kate.

Little Kate was his favorite; he put her in lead.
She had a keen nose and long legs, built for speed.
They all tugged at the snow hook, while Tom stilled
  the fuss,
Whispering, "Christmas in Nome is depending on us."

Tom attached a bright light to the top of his sled
For Santa to track from his sleigh overhead.
Tom's command "Okay, hike!" unleashed a great
    cry.
Eight tongues were a-flapping; eight tails lifted
    high.

Down the trail, they all blasted, a blistering
    pace.
And in time, Tom was blinded; snow
    swirled in his face.
His eyes, how they squinted; gee or haw, he
    knew not.
Tom counted on Kate through the freezing
    onslaught.

Through overflow and o'er sea ice, though the trail
  was unseen,
Huskies pulled at the gangline, into harness they
  leaned.
Tom kicked from the runners; Kate kept the lines
  tight,
While faithful, above them, Nick followed the light.

Some two hours later, they pulled into Nome.
When his vision adjusted, Tom saw all the homes
And a figure alighting on roofs, one by one,
The bag of toys shrinking, until there were none.

In a blink, old St. Nicholas joined Tom on the ice,
Saying, "Just one more gift for a 'kid' who's been
  nice."
With a quick nod from Santa, Tom's sled went away.
In its place, a small twin of the famous red sleigh.

Back at home, Santa had quite a story to share
When his missus served tea and asked, "How'd you
    fare?"
"We nearly missed Nome, but with Tom we got to it."
"Through that blinding snow? Tell me, how did he
    do it?"

Santa laughed, oh so hard! From his eye squeezed a
    tear.
"With a miniature sleigh and eight tiny reindeer!"

Did You Know?

Dog-mushing is Alaska's state sport and was an important mode of transportation for hunters, miners, traders, and even mail carriers. When fur traders and gold miners arrived in the late 1800s, they learned that Alaskan huskies were well suited for pulling loads over long distances. They also discovered that the dogs instinctively love to run as much as retrievers love to retrieve. Races became popular.

Nome was the center of Alaskan sled-dog races in the early twentieth century, and the famed dogs Togo and Balto were in the kennel of Norwegian musher Leonhard Seppala. In 1925, many children in Nome were sick from a diphtheria epidemic. Twenty Alaskan mushers—Indian, Eskimo, and non-Native alike—with about 150 dogs formed a cross-country relay to rush lifesaving serum from the railroad line at Nenana across rivers and mountain ranges to reach Nome. The last of the lead dogs in the nonstop race to save lives, Togo and Balto became famous in the national newspapers and later toured the country as celebrities. A statue of Balto was erected in New York's Central Park, and his story has been retold in movies and books.

Today, two 1,000-mile races feature the strength and stamina of incredible dog athletes and their mushers. The Iditarod Trail Sled Dog Race begins on the first Saturday of every March and follows a historic trail from Anchorage to Nome. The Yukon Quest International Sled Dog Race is run each February with the starting line alternating between Fairbanks, Alaska, and Whitehorse, Yukon Territory. Both races attract top dogs, mushers, volunteers, fans, and media from all over the world.

Tom's teammates, except for Kate, were named after these famous mushers: Joe Redington, Sr.; Lance Mackey; Susan Butcher; Rick Swenson; Doug Swingley; Jeff King; and Martin Buser.

Mushing Terms

Bootie: A sock that protects a dog's feet from sharp ice and trail wear
Gangline: Strong rope running down the team connecting dogs to each other and to the sled
Gee: Command for right turn
Haw: Command for left turn
Hike!: Let's go!
Leader: An especially skilled dog at the front of the team
Overflow: Running water on top of frozen sea or river ice
Runners: Parts of the sled that slide on the snow; mushers stand on the back ends of the runners and hold onto the handlebow
Snow hook: Curved metal "anchor" for sled and team
Traces: Harnesses and all of the connecting rope
Wheel dog: Team position directly in front of the sled